The Effectiveness of Efforts Against ISIS in Iraq and Syria

Copyright Page

TITLE: The Effectiveness of Efforts Against ISIS in Iraq and Syria

1ST Edition

ISBN: 9798223559320

Table of Contents

The Effectiveness of Efforts Against ISIS in Iraq and Syria 1

Chapter 1: Operation Inherent Resolve: The U.S. Military Intervention Against ISIS in Iraq and Syria 2

Chapter 2: The Impact of Operation Inherent Resolve on Regional Stability in the Middle East 8

Chapter 3: The Role of the U.S. Military in Combating ISIS Propaganda and Recruitment Efforts.. 14

Chapter 4: The Effectiveness of Coalition Forces in Coordinating Efforts against ISIS in Iraq and Syria.. 19

Chapter 5: The Humanitarian Consequences of Operation Inherent Resolve on Displaced Populations in Iraq and Syria 24

Chapter 6: The Challenges Faced by the U.S. Military in Training and Equipping Local Security Forces in Iraq and Syria 29

Chapter 7: The Geopolitical Implications of Operation Inherent Resolve on U.S.-Russia Relations in the Region 34

Chapter 8: The Role of Aerial and Drone Strikes in the Success of Operation Inherent Resolve against ISIS 40

Chapter 9: The Strategies Employed by ISIS in Response to Operation Inherent Resolve... 45

Chapter 10: The Impact of Operation Inherent Resolve on Reconstruction and Stabilization Efforts in Post-ISIS Iraq and Syria .. 50

Chapter 11: The Legal and Ethical Considerations Surrounding the U.S. Military Intervention in Iraq and Syria during Operation Inherent Resolve 56

The Effectiveness of Efforts Against ISIS in Iraq and Syria

By Roberto Miguel Rodriguez

Chapter 1: Operation Inherent Resolve: The U.S. Military Intervention Against ISIS in Iraq and Syria

The Origins and Objectives of Operation Inherent Resolve

Operation Inherent Resolve, the U.S. military intervention against ISIS in Iraq and Syria, has had a profound impact on various aspects of the region. Understanding the origins and objectives of this operation is crucial for historians and those interested in its niches.

Operation Inherent Resolve was launched in response to the rapid expansion of the Islamic State of Iraq and Syria (ISIS) in 2014. The group's brutal tactics, territorial gains, and the threat it posed to regional stability necessitated immediate action. The primary objective of this operation was to defeat ISIS and restore peace and security to Iraq and Syria.

The U.S. military played a critical role in combating ISIS propaganda and recruitment efforts. Through strategic messaging and information operations, the U.S. sought to counter the extremist ideology propagated by ISIS and prevent its global spread. The effectiveness of these efforts and the coordination with coalition forces are of great interest to historians studying the impact on regional stability in the Middle East.

Operation Inherent Resolve also had significant humanitarian consequences, particularly on the displaced populations in Iraq and Syria. The military campaign aimed to minimize civilian casualties and provide humanitarian assistance to affected communities. However, challenges emerged as the operation progressed, and the extent of its success in protecting civilians is a topic worth exploring.

Training and equipping local security forces in Iraq and Syria posed unique challenges for the U.S. military. Historians can delve into the difficulties faced in building capable and sustainable local forces to ensure long-term stability in the region.

The geopolitical implications of Operation Inherent Resolve, particularly on U.S.-Russia relations, are of immense importance. The intervention created a complex dynamic between the two superpowers, impacting their strategic interests in the region. Understanding these implications can shed light on the evolving geopolitical landscape in the Middle East.

The strategies employed by ISIS in response to Operation Inherent Resolve are also intriguing. The group adapted its tactics, exploited new vulnerabilities, and sought to maintain relevance despite significant setbacks. Analyzing these strategies helps to understand the evolving nature of the conflict.

Operation Inherent Resolve not only aimed to defeat ISIS but also to contribute to the reconstruction and stabilization efforts in post-ISIS Iraq and Syria. Historians can assess the impact of the operation on these endeavors, analyzing the challenges faced and the progress made.

Finally, the legal and ethical considerations surrounding the U.S. military intervention in Iraq and Syria during Operation Inherent Resolve are subjects that warrant exploration. Historians can examine the justifications for intervention, the adherence to international law, and the ethical dilemmas faced by military personnel.

In conclusion, the subchapter on the origins and objectives of Operation Inherent Resolve provides a comprehensive overview of the operation's historical context and its various niches. Understanding these aspects is crucial for historians and those interested in the impact on regional stability, humanitarian consequences, military strategies, geopolitical implications, and legal and ethical considerations.

The Role of the U.S. Military in the Coalition against ISIS

The U.S. military has played a pivotal role in the coalition efforts against the Islamic State of Iraq and Syria (ISIS), also known as Daesh. This subchapter aims to examine the various dimensions of the U.S. military's involvement in the fight against ISIS and assess its effectiveness in achieving the coalition's objectives.

Operation Inherent Resolve: The U.S. Military Intervention Against ISIS in Iraq and Syria

Operation Inherent Resolve marked a significant turning point in the fight against ISIS. The U.S. military, alongside its coalition partners, launched extensive air and ground operations to degrade and ultimately defeat the terrorist group. By providing crucial air support and deploying special operations forces, the U.S. military played a key role in retaking strategic territories from ISIS, such as Mosul in Iraq and Raqqa in Syria.

The impact of Operation Inherent Resolve on regional stability in the Middle East

Operation Inherent Resolve not only aimed to defeat ISIS but also sought to restore stability in the Middle East. The U.S. military's efforts have helped weaken the terrorist organization, thereby reducing its ability to carry out attacks and destabilize the region. However, challenges such as the resurgence of ISIS and the complex dynamics between regional powers continue to pose obstacles to achieving long-term stability.

The role of the U.S. military in combating ISIS propaganda and recruitment efforts

Recognizing the importance of countering ISIS propaganda and recruitment, the U.S. military has actively engaged in information operations to undermine the group's narrative and disrupt its recruitment efforts. Through targeted messaging, psychological operations, and cooperation with local partners, the U.S. military has contributed to reducing the appeal and reach of ISIS propaganda.

The effectiveness of coalition forces in coordinating efforts against ISIS in Iraq and Syria

The U.S. military's participation in a multinational coalition against ISIS has facilitated coordination and cooperation among various partners. Joint planning, intelligence sharing, and synchronized military operations have bolstered the effectiveness of the coalition's efforts, enabling a more unified and comprehensive approach to combating ISIS.

The humanitarian consequences of Operation Inherent Resolve on displaced populations in Iraq and Syria

While Operation Inherent Resolve has made significant gains in countering ISIS, it has also resulted in significant humanitarian consequences, particularly for displaced populations in Iraq and Syria. The U.S. military, in coordination with humanitarian organizations, has provided vital assistance, including food, shelter, and medical aid, to those affected by the conflict. However, challenges remain in ensuring the long-term well-being and stability of these populations.

In conclusion, the U.S. military has played a crucial role in the coalition against ISIS, contributing to the degradation and defeat of the terrorist group. From military interventions to countering propaganda and supporting humanitarian efforts, the U.S. military's multifaceted involvement has had a significant impact on the fight against ISIS in Iraq and Syria. However, challenges persist, and it is essential for historians to continue assessing the effectiveness and consequences of Operation Inherent Resolve to inform future strategies and policies.

The Tactics and Strategies Employed by U.S. Forces in Iraq and Syria

Introduction:

The U.S. military intervention against ISIS in Iraq and Syria, known as Operation Inherent Resolve, required a comprehensive set of tactics and strategies to effectively combat the terrorist organization. This subchapter aims to provide historians with an overview of the key approaches employed by U.S. forces during this operation.

1. Counterinsurgency Operations:

U.S. forces implemented counterinsurgency tactics to disrupt and dismantle ISIS networks in Iraq and Syria. These operations involved a combination of intelligence gathering, targeted raids, and coordinated airstrikes to identify and eliminate high-value targets while minimizing collateral damage.

2. Training and Equipping Local Security Forces:

One of the challenges faced by the U.S. military was the need to build the capacity of local security forces in Iraq and Syria. The U.S. provided training, equipment, and advisory support to Iraqi Security Forces and Syrian Democratic Forces, enabling them to take the lead in the fight against ISIS. This approach aimed to empower local forces to secure and stabilize their own territories.

3. Special Operations:

U.S. special operations forces played a critical role in conducting high-risk missions, such as intelligence gathering, reconnaissance, and direct action against ISIS leaders. These elite forces operated in small teams, often working alongside local partners, to gather actionable intelligence and carry out precision strikes.

4. Aerial and Drone Strikes:

The use of aerial bombardment and drone strikes was a central component of the U.S. strategy in Operation Inherent Resolve. These strikes targeted ISIS command and control centers, training camps, and infrastructure, degrading the group's capabilities and disrupting its operations.

5. Cyber Warfare and Propaganda Countermeasures:

Recognizing the importance of countering ISIS propaganda and recruitment efforts, the U.S. military employed cyber warfare capabilities to disrupt the group's online presence. This involved targeting social media accounts, websites, and communication networks used by ISIS to spread its ideology and recruit followers.

Conclusion:

The tactics and strategies employed by U.S. forces in Iraq and Syria during Operation Inherent Resolve were multifaceted and aimed at combating ISIS from various angles. The integration of counterinsurgency operations, training and equipping local forces, special operations, aerial and drone strikes, and cyber warfare showcased the complexity of the U.S. military's approach. By employing these strategies, the U.S. achieved significant successes in degrading ISIS capabilities and reclaiming territory in Iraq and Syria. However, the challenges faced by the U.S. military in training local forces, navigating geopolitical complexities, and addressing humanitarian consequences highlight the need for a comprehensive assessment of the operation's overall effectiveness.

Chapter 2: The Impact of Operation Inherent Resolve on Regional Stability in the Middle East

The Political and Social Dynamics in Iraq and Syria Pre-Intervention

Before delving into the effectiveness of the coalition forces' efforts against ISIS in Iraq and Syria, it is crucial to understand the political and social dynamics that set the stage for intervention. This subchapter aims to provide historians with an in-depth analysis of the complex landscape that existed prior to Operation Inherent Resolve.

In both Iraq and Syria, political and social tensions had been simmering for years, creating a fertile ground for the rise of ISIS. In Iraq, the sectarian divide between the Sunni and Shia populations had been exacerbated by the power vacuum left by the U.S. invasion in 2003. The Sunni minority felt marginalized by the Shia-dominated government, leading to widespread disillusionment and support for extremist groups like ISIS.

Syria, on the other hand, experienced a similar power struggle between the regime of Bashar al-Assad and various opposition groups. As the Syrian civil war unfolded, ISIS capitalized on the chaos and established its self-proclaimed caliphate, attracting disenchanted Syrians and foreign fighters alike.

These political and social dynamics were further complicated by regional rivalries and external influences. Iran, a Shia-majority country, supported the Assad regime in Syria, while countries like Saudi Arabia and Turkey backed various opposition groups. This proxy war not only prolonged the conflict but also provided an opportunity for ISIS to expand its reach.

The subchapter also explores the impact of these pre-intervention dynamics on regional stability in the Middle East. The rise of ISIS posed a direct threat to neighboring countries, as well as to global security. The group's territorial gains and recruitment efforts fueled instability, leading to a mass displacement of populations and exacerbating humanitarian crises.

Historians will gain insights into the strategies employed by ISIS in response to Operation Inherent Resolve, as well as the legal and ethical considerations surrounding the U.S. military intervention. The chapter will also touch upon the challenges faced by the U.S. military in training and equipping local security forces in Iraq and Syria.

By thoroughly examining the political and social dynamics that existed prior to intervention, historians can better understand the context in which Operation Inherent Resolve unfolded. This understanding is crucial for assessing the effectiveness of the coalition forces' efforts against ISIS and drawing lessons for future counterterrorism operations.

The Ripple Effects of Operation Inherent Resolve on Neighboring Countries

Operation Inherent Resolve, the U.S. military intervention against ISIS in Iraq and Syria, has had far-reaching consequences on the neighboring countries in the Middle East. This subchapter delves into the various ripple effects that have been observed as a result of this operation.

One of the primary concerns surrounding Operation Inherent Resolve is its impact on regional stability in the Middle East. Historians have closely examined the implications of the U.S. military intervention on neighboring countries such as Turkey, Jordan, and Lebanon. The influx of displaced populations seeking refuge in these countries has strained their resources and infrastructure, disrupting the delicate balance in the region.

Another crucial aspect to consider is the role of the U.S. military in combating ISIS propaganda and recruitment efforts. By analyzing the effectiveness of their strategies, historians can gain insights into the impact of Operation Inherent Resolve on countering extremist ideologies. This subchapter explores the tactics employed by the U.S. military to disrupt ISIS's recruitment networks and propaganda machinery.

Furthermore, a critical assessment of the effectiveness of coalition forces in coordinating efforts against ISIS in Iraq and Syria is essential. Historians have closely examined the challenges faced by the diverse coalition in terms of communication, strategy, and resource allocation. By understanding these dynamics, valuable lessons can be learned for future military interventions.

The humanitarian consequences of Operation Inherent Resolve cannot be overlooked. The displacement of populations in Iraq and Syria has resulted in a significant humanitarian crisis. This subchapter addresses the challenges faced by displaced populations and the efforts made by the international community to provide aid and support.

Moreover, historians have closely analyzed the challenges faced by the U.S. military in training and equipping local security forces in Iraq and Syria. This subchapter explores the obstacles encountered and the strategies implemented to enhance the capabilities of local forces.

The geopolitical implications of Operation Inherent Resolve on U.S.-Russia relations in the region are also examined. Historians assess the impact of this operation on the complex relationship between these two major powers and its broader implications for regional stability.

Additionally, the role of aerial and drone strikes in the success of Operation Inherent Resolve against ISIS is analyzed. Historians evaluate the effectiveness and ethical considerations surrounding these tactics.

Furthermore, this subchapter explores the strategies employed by ISIS in response to Operation Inherent Resolve, including their adaptive tactics and attempts to regroup and regain control.

Lastly, the impact of Operation Inherent Resolve on the reconstruction and stabilization efforts in post-ISIS Iraq and Syria is examined. Historians assess the progress made in rebuilding infrastructure, restoring governance, and providing essential services to the affected regions.

Throughout this subchapter, legal and ethical considerations surrounding the U.S. military intervention in Iraq and Syria during Operation Inherent Resolve are carefully examined. Historians analyze the justifications for intervention, adherence to international law, and the ethical implications of military actions.

By addressing these topics, this subchapter provides historians with a comprehensive understanding of the ripple effects of Operation Inherent Resolve on neighboring countries. It offers valuable insights into the complexities of military interventions, regional stability, humanitarian consequences, and geopolitical implications in the Middle East.

The Influence of Operation Inherent Resolve on Extremist Movements in the Region

Operation Inherent Resolve, the U.S. military intervention against ISIS in Iraq and Syria, has had a significant influence on extremist movements in the region. This subchapter will explore the various ways in which this operation has impacted the landscape of extremism in the Middle East.

One of the key aspects to consider is the impact of Operation Inherent Resolve on regional stability in the Middle East. Historians can examine how the intervention has disrupted extremist networks and hindered their ability to carry out attacks. By targeting key ISIS strongholds and infrastructure, coalition forces have weakened the organization's capabilities and reduced its territorial control. This has resulted in a decline in extremist activities, contributing to enhanced regional stability.

Furthermore, the role of the U.S. military in combating ISIS propaganda and recruitment efforts cannot be underestimated. Through targeted airstrikes and ground operations, coalition forces have not only disrupted ISIS's ability to spread its ideology but also hindered its recruitment efforts. Historians can analyze the strategies employed by the U.S. military to counter ISIS's online presence, including monitoring and disrupting their social media platforms and online networks.

The effectiveness of coalition forces in coordinating efforts against ISIS in Iraq and Syria is another crucial aspect to explore. Historians can delve into the challenges faced by the coalition in terms of coordination, communication, and sharing intelligence. By evaluating the successes and failures of coalition coordination, valuable lessons can be learned for future military interventions against extremist organizations.

Operation Inherent Resolve has also had humanitarian consequences on displaced populations in Iraq and Syria. The subchapter can examine the challenges faced by these populations, including the displacement of millions, the destruction of infrastructure, and the loss of livelihoods. Historians can analyze the efforts made by coalition forces to provide humanitarian aid and support to these affected populations, as well as the long-term implications of the intervention on their lives.

Moreover, the subchapter can address the challenges faced by the U.S. military in training and equipping local security forces in Iraq and Syria. Historians can assess the effectiveness of these efforts in building capable and sustainable security forces that can maintain stability in the post-ISIS era.

Lastly, the geopolitical implications of Operation Inherent Resolve on U.S.-Russia relations in the region cannot be overlooked. Historians can analyze how the intervention has affected the delicate balance of power between these two global powers and the subsequent implications for regional stability.

In conclusion, Operation Inherent Resolve has had a profound influence on extremist movements in the region. Historians can explore the multiple dimensions of this impact, including its effect on regional stability, the role of the U.S. military in countering propaganda and recruitment efforts, the effectiveness of coalition coordination, the humanitarian consequences, the challenges faced in training local security forces, the geopolitical implications, and the legal and ethical considerations surrounding the intervention.

Chapter 3: The Role of the U.S. Military in Combating ISIS Propaganda and Recruitment Efforts

Psychological Warfare: Counteracting ISIS Propaganda

In the battle against ISIS, one of the most critical fronts is the psychological warfare being waged by the terrorist organization. ISIS has been highly effective in using propaganda to recruit new members and spread fear and chaos in the region. To counteract these efforts, coalition forces engaged in Operation Inherent Resolve have recognized the urgent need to dismantle the ISIS propaganda machine.

Understanding the power of propaganda, coalition forces have developed a comprehensive strategy to counter ISIS messaging. The first step in this strategy is to disrupt the dissemination of propaganda materials by targeting key communication channels. This includes taking down social media accounts, websites, and other online platforms that serve as recruitment and propaganda hubs for ISIS.

In addition to disrupting their online presence, coalition forces have launched a vigorous campaign to expose the falsehoods and contradictions within ISIS propaganda. By highlighting the atrocities committed by the terrorist organization and showcasing the realities of life under ISIS rule, efforts are being made to dissuade potential recruits and undermine the credibility of the organization.

To counteract ISIS propaganda, coalition forces have also focused on promoting positive narratives and offering alternative messages to vulnerable populations. This includes showcasing success stories of individuals who have rejected ISIS and chosen a different path. By emphasizing the benefits of peace, stability, and inclusivity, coalition forces aim to counter the allure of radicalization.

Moreover, coalition forces have collaborated with local communities, religious leaders, and influential figures to amplify these counter-narratives. By empowering local voices to speak out against ISIS and promote alternative ideologies, the effectiveness of the messaging is enhanced.

While progress has been made in countering ISIS propaganda, challenges remain. ISIS continues to adapt and evolve its messaging strategies, utilizing encrypted communication channels and exploiting the vulnerabilities of social media platforms. Coalition forces must remain vigilant and adaptive in their efforts to counteract these evolving tactics.

In conclusion, psychological warfare plays a crucial role in the fight against ISIS. By dismantling their propaganda machine, exposing their falsehoods, and promoting positive alternatives, coalition forces are working to counteract the influence of ISIS and disrupt their recruitment efforts. Through collaboration with local communities and influential figures, these counter-narratives can have a lasting impact on the stability and security of the region. The ongoing commitment to this psychological warfare is imperative in the broader mission of Operation Inherent Resolve.

Disrupting Recruitment Networks: Efforts and Challenges

Recruitment has been a crucial aspect of ISIS' strategy to build a formidable force in Iraq and Syria. To counter this threat, coalition forces, led by the United States, have made significant efforts to disrupt the recruitment networks of the terrorist organization. However, these efforts have faced numerous challenges, both operational and strategic.

One of the key challenges in disrupting recruitment networks is the decentralized nature of ISIS' operations. The organization has been able to adapt quickly and establish new recruitment channels in response to previous disruptions. The coalition forces have had to constantly identify and target these new networks, which requires a high level of intelligence gathering and coordination among the coalition partners.

Another challenge has been the use of social media and online platforms by ISIS for recruitment purposes. The organization has exploited the internet to disseminate propaganda and attract vulnerable individuals to join its ranks. While the coalition has made efforts to counter this online presence, the sheer volume of online content and the speed at which it can spread make it difficult to completely eliminate this recruitment avenue.

Furthermore, local support for ISIS in certain areas has hindered the effectiveness of disruption efforts. In some cases, local populations have been reluctant to cooperate with coalition forces due to fear of retaliation or lack of trust. This has made it challenging to gather intelligence and identify key individuals involved in recruitment networks.

Additionally, the flow of foreign fighters to Iraq and Syria has posed a significant challenge. Many individuals from various countries have traveled to the region to join ISIS, making it difficult to track and disrupt these recruitment networks on an international scale. The coalition forces have had to work closely with intelligence agencies and partner countries to share information and prevent the movement of foreign fighters.

Despite these challenges, the coalition forces have achieved some success in disrupting recruitment networks. Through targeted airstrikes, raids, and intelligence sharing, they have been able to dismantle key nodes in the recruitment chain. By disrupting the flow of new recruits, the coalition has made it more difficult for ISIS to replenish its ranks and maintain its strength.

However, it is important to recognize that disrupting recruitment networks alone is not sufficient to defeat ISIS. The organization's ability to adapt and evolve means that efforts must also focus on countering its ideology, addressing the root causes of radicalization, and promoting stability and development in the region.

In conclusion, disrupting recruitment networks has been a critical aspect of the coalition's efforts against ISIS in Iraq and Syria. Despite the challenges posed by decentralized operations, online propaganda, local support, and foreign fighters, the coalition forces have made significant progress in disrupting these networks. However, a comprehensive approach that addresses the underlying causes of radicalization and promotes stability is necessary to fully counter the threat of ISIS.

Media Engagement: Shaping the Narrative against ISIS

In the fight against ISIS, media engagement has emerged as a critical tool in shaping the narrative and countering the extremist group's propaganda and recruitment efforts. This subchapter focuses on the role of media engagement in the broader context of the coalition's efforts against ISIS in Iraq and Syria.

The media landscape has drastically changed in recent years, and ISIS has effectively exploited these platforms to spread its extremist ideology and recruit vulnerable individuals. Recognizing the power of media, coalition forces have strategically employed various tactics to counter ISIS's messaging and undermine its influence.

One of the key strategies employed by the coalition has been to engage and empower local communities and religious leaders to challenge ISIS's narrative. By amplifying the voices of moderate Muslims and highlighting their efforts to counter extremism, the coalition has sought to delegitimize ISIS and offer alternative narratives that resonate with vulnerable populations.

Furthermore, the coalition has established media centers and partnered with local media outlets to disseminate accurate and timely information. Through these channels, they have aimed to expose the true nature of ISIS and debunk its propaganda. This approach has been particularly effective in reaching audiences within the region and countering ISIS's online recruitment efforts.

Additionally, the coalition has leveraged social media platforms to directly engage with individuals at risk of radicalization. By providing alternative narratives, promoting positive messages, and offering support, they have sought to dissuade individuals from joining or supporting ISIS.

However, media engagement comes with its own set of challenges. The coalition has had to navigate issues of cultural sensitivity, language barriers, and misinformation, all while ensuring the accuracy and credibility of the information disseminated.

This subchapter will critically analyze the effectiveness of these media engagement efforts in countering ISIS's narrative and recruitment efforts. It will also explore the ethical considerations surrounding the use of media as a weapon in the fight against terrorism.

By examining the various media strategies employed by the coalition, this subchapter aims to provide historians and experts with a comprehensive understanding of the role of media engagement in shaping the narrative against ISIS. It will also shed light on the challenges faced and lessons learned in countering extremist propaganda, ultimately contributing to the broader assessment of the effectiveness of coalition efforts against ISIS in Iraq and Syria.

Chapter 4: The Effectiveness of Coalition Forces in Coordinating Efforts against ISIS in Iraq and Syria

The Challenges of Coalition Coordination: Lessons Learned

In the complex and multifaceted fight against ISIS in Iraq and Syria, coalition coordination has proven to be a daunting task. The lessons learned from this endeavor have shed light on the numerous challenges faced by the participating nations. This subchapter aims to delve into these challenges and provide insights for historians and specialists interested in understanding the intricacies of coalition operations.

One of the primary challenges encountered during the coalition effort was the coordination of diverse military forces operating in Iraq and Syria. With each nation bringing its own set of strategies, tactics, and rules of engagement, achieving a unified front was no small feat. Differences in command structures, communication systems, and cultural approaches to warfare often hindered seamless cooperation.

Additionally, the ever-changing nature of the conflict posed significant challenges. ISIS employed adaptive tactics and morphing strategies to counter coalition efforts. As a result, coalition forces had to constantly reassess and adapt their own strategies to effectively combat the terrorist group. The need for flexible and agile decision-making processes became apparent, as the success of coalition efforts hinged on the ability to swiftly respond to the evolving threat landscape.

Another critical challenge faced by the coalition was the coordination of humanitarian efforts alongside military operations. The fight against ISIS resulted in large-scale displacement and significant humanitarian crises in Iraq and Syria. Balancing the need to provide aid and support to affected populations while simultaneously conducting military operations was a complex task. The coordination of humanitarian agencies, military forces, and local actors was essential to mitigate the impact on displaced populations and ensure their safety and well-being.

Furthermore, the legal and ethical considerations surrounding the military intervention in Iraq and Syria added another layer of complexity to coalition coordination. Striking a balance between the imperative to combat ISIS and the need to adhere to international law and ethical standards posed significant challenges. Ensuring that military actions were proportionate, avoiding civilian casualties, and respecting the sovereignty of host nations required careful deliberation and coordination among coalition partners.

In conclusion, the challenges of coalition coordination in the fight against ISIS in Iraq and Syria have been multifaceted and demanding. The lessons learned from this experience highlight the importance of effective communication, flexible decision-making, and the ability to adapt to the evolving threat landscape. Moreover, the coordination of humanitarian efforts and adherence to legal and ethical standards proved to be critical in mitigating the impact on displaced populations and maintaining the legitimacy of the coalition intervention. By understanding and addressing these challenges, future coalition efforts can be more effectively coordinated, leading to greater success in combating extremist groups and fostering stability in the Middle East.

Assessing the Successes and Failures of Coalition Operations

Introduction:

The subchapter titled "Assessing the Successes and Failures of Coalition Operations" delves into the evaluation of the effectiveness of coalition efforts against ISIS in Iraq and Syria. This section aims to provide a comprehensive analysis for historians and experts in various niches, focusing on Operation Inherent Resolve and its broader implications.

By critically examining the achievements and shortcomings of coalition forces, this subchapter sheds light on the multifaceted nature of the military intervention and its impact on regional stability, humanitarian consequences, counter-propaganda efforts, and more.

Assessing Coalition Effectiveness:

1. Military Coordination: The subchapter begins by evaluating the effectiveness of coalition forces in coordinating efforts against ISIS in Iraq and Syria. It examines the challenges faced by the coalition, such as divergent military strategies, communication barriers, and the integration of various national forces. Additionally, it analyses successful instances of collaboration and highlights areas that require further improvement.

2. Humanitarian Consequences: This section explores the humanitarian consequences of Operation Inherent Resolve on displaced populations in Iraq and Syria. It examines the impact of military operations on civilians, including displacement, casualties, and the destruction of infrastructure. It also evaluates the effectiveness of coalition forces in providing humanitarian aid and addressing the needs of affected populations.

3. Counter-Propaganda Efforts: The role of the U.S. military in combating ISIS propaganda and recruitment efforts is closely examined. This section assesses the effectiveness of various strategies employed to counter extremist narratives, including social media campaigns, psychological operations, and local partnerships. It also discusses the challenges faced and identifies areas for improvement.

4. Training and Equipping Local Security Forces: The subchapter investigates the challenges faced by the U.S. military in training and equipping local security forces in Iraq and Syria. It evaluates the impact of these efforts on the effectiveness of local forces in combating ISIS

and maintaining stability in the region. The section also examines the sustainability and long-term implications of these training programs.

5. Geopolitical Implications: This section explores the geopolitical implications of Operation Inherent Resolve on U.S.-Russia relations in the region. It analyzes the complexities of the regional power dynamics and the interaction between the coalition, Russia, and other regional actors. The subchapter assesses the impact of the military intervention on broader geopolitical interests.

Conclusion:

The subchapter titled "Assessing the Successes and Failures of Coalition Operations" provides historians and experts with a comprehensive evaluation of the effectiveness of coalition efforts against ISIS in Iraq and Syria. By examining military coordination, humanitarian consequences, counter-propaganda efforts, training and equipping local forces, and geopolitical implications, this section offers a nuanced understanding of Operation Inherent Resolve and its multifaceted impact. Through this analysis, historians can gain insights into the successes and failures of coalition operations and their broader implications for regional stability, humanitarian concerns, geopolitical dynamics, and ethical considerations.

The Role of Intelligence Sharing in the Fight against ISIS

Intelligence sharing has played a crucial role in the fight against ISIS during Operation Inherent Resolve. This subchapter will delve into the significance of intelligence sharing among coalition forces, highlighting its impact on the overall effectiveness of efforts against ISIS in Iraq and Syria.

The sharing of intelligence has been a cornerstone of coalition coordination, enabling member countries to pool their resources and knowledge to counter the threats posed by ISIS. Historically, intelligence sharing has been essential in military operations, and combating ISIS has been no exception. The complex and adaptive nature of the terrorist organization requires constant surveillance and monitoring, which can only be achieved through effective intelligence sharing.

By sharing intelligence, coalition forces have been able to identify and target key ISIS leaders, disrupt their communication networks, and dismantle their infrastructure. This has been critical in weakening the organization and reducing its ability to carry out large-scale attacks. Moreover, intelligence sharing has facilitated the tracking and apprehension of foreign fighters, preventing them from returning to their home countries and potentially carrying out acts of terrorism.

The impact of intelligence sharing on regional stability in the Middle East cannot be overstated. By working together and exchanging vital information, coalition forces have been able to prevent the spread of ISIS influence beyond Iraq and Syria. This has curtailed the organization's ability to establish new strongholds and recruit new members, ultimately contributing to regional stability.

However, intelligence sharing is not without its challenges. Various factors, such as differing national interests and concerns over the protection of sensitive information, can hinder effective collaboration. Overcoming these challenges requires trust, transparency, and a shared commitment to the common goal of defeating ISIS.

In conclusion, intelligence sharing has been instrumental in the fight against ISIS during Operation Inherent Resolve. By pooling their resources and knowledge, coalition forces have been able to disrupt the organization's activities, prevent the spread of its influence, and enhance regional stability. While challenges exist, the importance of intelligence sharing cannot be underestimated in the ongoing efforts to combat terrorism and ensure a safer future for Iraq, Syria, and the entire Middle East region.

Chapter 5: The Humanitarian Consequences of Operation Inherent Resolve on Displaced Populations in Iraq and Syria

The Plight of Internally Displaced Persons (IDPs) in Iraq and Syria

The conflicts in Iraq and Syria, particularly during the rise and fall of ISIS, have resulted in a significant number of internally displaced persons (IDPs) in both countries. These individuals, who have been forced to flee their homes due to violence, persecution, and the destruction of their communities, face numerous challenges and hardships.

In Iraq, the number of IDPs reached staggering proportions, with estimates suggesting that over 3 million people were displaced during the height of the conflict. Similarly, Syria witnessed a mass exodus of its population, with millions of people seeking refuge within the country or across its borders. This displacement crisis has had far-reaching humanitarian consequences, placing immense strain on the resources and capacities of host communities and aid organizations.

IDPs face numerous challenges in their daily lives, including limited access to basic necessities such as food, water, healthcare, and education. Many find themselves living in overcrowded and inadequate shelters, often lacking proper sanitation facilities and security. The psychological toll of displacement is also significant, with many individuals suffering from trauma and post-traumatic stress disorder.

The international community, including organizations such as the United Nations and non-governmental organizations, has been working diligently to provide assistance and support to IDPs. However, due to the scale of the crisis and the ongoing security challenges in the region, these efforts have often fallen short of addressing the needs of all those affected.

Furthermore, the plight of IDPs has been exacerbated by the complex and dynamic nature of the conflicts in Iraq and Syria. The fluid frontlines and shifting allegiances have made it difficult for aid organizations to access and provide assistance to those in need. Moreover, the destruction of infrastructure and the presence of explosive remnants of war have hindered the safe return of IDPs to their homes.

Addressing the needs of IDPs is not only a humanitarian imperative but also crucial for the long-term stability and reconstruction of Iraq and Syria. It is essential for the international community, including the United States and its coalition partners, to prioritize the protection and assistance of IDPs. This includes ensuring their safety, providing them with access to essential services, and supporting their durable solutions, such as voluntary return, local integration, or resettlement.

In conclusion, the plight of IDPs in Iraq and Syria is a pressing issue that demands attention and action from historians and other stakeholders interested in the conflicts in the region. By understanding the challenges faced by IDPs, we can better appreciate the complexities of the conflicts and the importance of addressing the humanitarian consequences of these conflicts.

Humanitarian Aid Efforts: Successes and Obstacles

One of the key aspects of any military intervention is the provision of humanitarian aid to the affected populations. In the case of Operation Inherent Resolve, the U.S. military intervention against ISIS in Iraq and Syria, humanitarian aid efforts have played a crucial role in mitigating the impact of the conflict on the displaced populations and supporting the overall stabilization and reconstruction efforts in the region.

The successes of the humanitarian aid efforts can be attributed to the coordination and collaboration among the coalition forces. The establishment of the Global Coalition to Defeat ISIS provided a platform for the participating countries to pool their resources and expertise in delivering aid to those in need. This coordination allowed for a more efficient and effective response, ensuring that the aid reached the affected populations in a timely manner.

Furthermore, the U.S. military played a significant role in combating ISIS propaganda and recruitment efforts. By working closely with local communities and leveraging their intelligence capabilities, the U.S. military was able to disrupt the communication channels and dismantle the recruitment networks of the terrorist organization. This not only prevented further radicalization but also contributed to the overall stability in the region.

However, despite these successes, there were significant obstacles that impeded the delivery of humanitarian aid. The volatile security situation in Iraq and Syria posed a major challenge, as the conflict zones were often inaccessible or too dangerous for aid convoys to reach. The presence of ISIS and other extremist groups also hindered the efforts of humanitarian organizations, which faced threats and attacks from these groups.

Moreover, the displacement of populations due to the conflict resulted in overcrowded refugee camps and strained resources. Providing adequate shelter, food, and medical assistance to the displaced populations proved to be a daunting task for the humanitarian organizations involved. The lack of funding and resources further exacerbated the challenges faced in meeting the basic needs of the affected populations.

In conclusion, the humanitarian aid efforts in Operation Inherent Resolve have had both successes and obstacles. The coordination among the coalition forces and the efforts in combating ISIS propaganda have yielded positive results in supporting the affected populations and stabilizing the region. However, the volatile security situation and the strain on resources have posed significant challenges in delivering aid to those in need. Despite these obstacles, the humanitarian aid efforts continue to play a crucial role in the overall success of the military intervention and the subsequent reconstruction and stabilization efforts in post-ISIS Iraq and Syria.

Addressing the Long-Term Challenges of Reconstruction and Refugee Return

As historians examine the multifaceted aspects of Operation Inherent Resolve, it is crucial to delve into the long-term challenges of reconstruction and refugee return in post-ISIS Iraq and Syria. This subchapter aims to shed light on the complex issues surrounding these critical areas and their implications for regional stability in the Middle East.

The aftermath of conflict often leaves a trail of destruction, and the situation in Iraq and Syria is no exception. Reconstructing cities ravaged by the brutal reign of ISIS requires a comprehensive approach that encompasses physical infrastructure, social services, and economic revitalization. Historically, successful reconstruction efforts have relied on international collaboration, with the United States playing a prominent role. Understanding the challenges faced by the U.S. military in training and equipping local security forces is crucial in assessing the effectiveness of these efforts.

Another key concern is the refugee crisis stemming from the conflict. Operation Inherent Resolve has displaced millions of individuals, both internally and externally. Addressing the humanitarian consequences of this displacement is essential to ensure the protection and well-being of affected populations. Historians must analyze the strategies employed by

ISIS in response to Operation Inherent Resolve, particularly regarding the displacement of civilians, to gain a comprehensive understanding of the challenges faced.

Furthermore, the impact of Operation Inherent Resolve on the reconstruction and stabilization efforts in post-ISIS Iraq and Syria cannot be underestimated. The success of these efforts is integral to regional stability in the Middle East. Historians should explore the geopolitical implications of the operation on U.S.-Russia relations in the region, as well as the legal and ethical considerations surrounding the U.S. military intervention during Operation Inherent Resolve.

Lastly, it is crucial to assess the effectiveness of coalition forces in coordinating efforts against ISIS in Iraq and Syria. Examining the role of aerial and drone strikes in the success of Operation Inherent Resolve against ISIS will provide valuable insights into the military strategies employed.

In conclusion, addressing the long-term challenges of reconstruction and refugee return is vital to understanding the broader implications of Operation Inherent Resolve. Historians must scrutinize the impact of the operation on regional stability, the strategies employed by ISIS, and the legal and ethical considerations surrounding the intervention. By doing so, a comprehensive assessment of the effectiveness of coalition forces and the humanitarian consequences of the operation can be achieved. Only through a holistic understanding of these issues can lessons be learned and future interventions be better informed.

Chapter 6: The Challenges Faced by the U.S. Military in Training and Equipping Local Security Forces in Iraq and Syria

The Need for Local Partners: Building Effective Security Forces

In the fight against ISIS in Iraq and Syria, one crucial aspect that cannot be overlooked is the need for local partners in building effective security forces. This subchapter aims to highlight the significance of local partnerships and their role in the success of Operation Inherent Resolve.

One of the key lessons learned from previous military interventions is the importance of working closely with local actors. Historians have observed that successful military campaigns often require the support and cooperation of local forces who possess a deep understanding of the region's dynamics, culture, and terrain. This is especially true in the case of Operation Inherent Resolve, where local partners have played a critical role in countering ISIS and restoring stability in Iraq and Syria.

By collaborating with local security forces, the coalition has been able to leverage their knowledge and expertise, enhancing the effectiveness of military operations. Local partners have proven invaluable in gathering intelligence, identifying ISIS strongholds, and disrupting their logistical networks. Their familiarity with the local population has also facilitated the development of targeted strategies to counter ISIS propaganda and recruitment efforts.

Furthermore, building effective security forces at the local level is essential for long-term stability in the region. The coalition has recognized the need to train and equip local partners to ensure they can independently address security challenges and prevent the resurgence of extremist groups. However, this endeavor has not been without its challenges.

The U.S. military has faced numerous obstacles in training and equipping local security forces. Limited resources, language barriers, and a complex political landscape have posed significant challenges. Nonetheless, efforts have been made to address these challenges through increased coordination, capacity building, and the provision of necessary equipment.

The success of Operation Inherent Resolve hinges on the ability to establish strong local partnerships. By working closely with local security forces, the coalition can better understand the nuances of the region and tailor its strategies accordingly. These partnerships not only enhance military effectiveness but also contribute to long-term stability in Iraq and Syria.

In conclusion, the need for local partners in building effective security forces cannot be overstated. Historians studying Operation Inherent Resolve will recognize the pivotal role played by local actors in countering ISIS and restoring stability in the region. Through collaboration, training, and equipping, the coalition has been able to leverage the strengths of local partners, contributing to the overall success of the military intervention. Looking ahead, continued support for local security forces will be crucial in sustaining the gains made and preventing the resurgence of extremist groups in post-ISIS Iraq and Syria.

Overcoming Obstacles in Training and Capacity Building

In the fight against ISIS in Iraq and Syria, training and capacity building have emerged as crucial components of coalition efforts. The success of Operation Inherent Resolve hinges on the ability to equip local security forces and empower them to effectively combat the terrorist group. However, this process has not been without its obstacles.

One of the primary obstacles faced by the U.S. military in training and equipping local security forces is the lack of infrastructure and resources in Iraq and Syria. Years of conflict and instability have left these countries with weakened institutions and a shortage of trained personnel. This poses a challenge to coalition forces as they strive to build capable and sustainable security forces.

Another significant obstacle is the language and cultural barriers that exist between coalition forces and local populations. Effective training requires clear communication and understanding, but overcoming language barriers can be time-consuming and challenging. Cultural differences also play a role in training, as coalition forces must navigate local customs and traditions to build trust and rapport with their trainees.

Furthermore, the security situation in Iraq and Syria remains volatile, with ongoing insurgent attacks and pockets of ISIS resistance. This poses a threat to the training process, as trainees may be targeted or forced to abandon their training due to security concerns. The constant need for security measures diverts resources and attention away from the training and capacity-building efforts.

To overcome these obstacles, coalition forces have implemented several strategies. Firstly, they have increased their presence and engagement with local communities, aiming to establish trust and gather intelligence on potential threats. This approach helps to bridge the cultural divide and ensure that training efforts are tailored to local needs and realities.

Additionally, coalition forces have collaborated with international partners and non-governmental organizations to leverage their expertise in training and capacity building. This cooperation allows for the sharing of best practices and the pooling of resources, enhancing the effectiveness of training programs.

Moreover, the use of technology and innovation has played a significant role in overcoming obstacles. Virtual training platforms and simulators have been employed to provide realistic and immersive training experiences, mitigating the challenges posed by limited resources and infrastructure.

In conclusion, while the training and capacity-building efforts in Operation Inherent Resolve face numerous obstacles, coalition forces have demonstrated resilience and adaptability in addressing these challenges. By establishing trust with local communities, collaborating with international partners, and leveraging technology, they are working towards building capable and sustainable security forces in Iraq and Syria. Overcoming these obstacles is crucial not only for the success of the mission but also for the long-term stability and security of the region.

Balancing Interests: Navigating Regional Power Dynamics

The subchapter "Balancing Interests: Navigating Regional Power Dynamics" explores the complex dynamics and challenges faced by the coalition forces involved in Operation Inherent Resolve, as they combat the threat of ISIS in Iraq and Syria. This section delves into the intricate web of regional power dynamics and the delicate balancing act required to navigate them effectively.

Throughout history, the Middle East has been a region of significant geopolitical importance, characterized by competing interests and rivalries among regional powers. Operation Inherent Resolve, initiated by the U.S. military, aimed to not only counter the threat of ISIS but also maintain regional stability in the Middle East. However, achieving this delicate balance proved to be a formidable task.

One of the key challenges faced by the coalition forces was the need to collaborate and coordinate efforts with various regional actors, each with their own vested interests. Historically strained relationships, such as those between the U.S. and Iran, or Turkey and the Kurdish forces, further complicated the situation. The subchapter examines the strategies employed by the coalition forces to navigate these power dynamics, seeking to find common ground and shared objectives.

Moreover, the subchapter delves into the impact of these power dynamics on the effectiveness of the coalition forces. The competing interests and divergent agendas among regional actors often impeded the coordination of efforts against ISIS. Additionally, these dynamics affected the distribution of resources, intelligence sharing, and the overall military strategy employed in the region.

Furthermore, the subchapter explores the implications of Operation Inherent Resolve on U.S.-Russia relations in the region. The involvement of Russia in the Syrian conflict added another layer of complexity to the regional power dynamics. The subchapter analyzes how the U.S. military navigated this relationship and the broader geopolitical implications it had on the region.

Ultimately, "Balancing Interests: Navigating Regional Power Dynamics" sheds light on the intricacies of coalition coordination in the fight against ISIS. It provides historians with a comprehensive understanding of the challenges faced by the coalition forces and the strategies employed to balance regional power dynamics. This subchapter serves as a valuable resource for those interested in understanding the multifaceted nature of Operation Inherent Resolve and its impact on regional stability in the Middle East.

Chapter 7: The Geopolitical Implications of Operation Inherent Resolve on U.S.-Russia Relations in the Region

U.S.-Russia Rivalry in Iraq and Syria: Cooperation or Confrontation?

The U.S.-Russia rivalry in Iraq and Syria during Operation Inherent Resolve has been a topic of great interest and concern for historians studying the complex dynamics of the conflict. Both countries have been key players in the fight against ISIS, but their differing approaches and strategic objectives have often led to tensions and potential confrontations.

On one hand, there have been instances of limited cooperation between the U.S. and Russia in their efforts against ISIS. For example, both countries have conducted airstrikes against the terrorist group and have shared intelligence to some extent. This cooperation, although limited, has demonstrated a willingness to put aside differences for the sake of a common goal – eradicating ISIS from the region.

However, it is important to note that the U.S. and Russia have fundamentally different visions for the future of Iraq and Syria. The U.S. has supported various rebel groups in Syria and has called for the removal of President Bashar al-Assad, while Russia has provided military assistance to the Syrian government and has actively supported Assad's regime. This stark divergence in objectives has often led to confrontations, both on the ground and diplomatically.

The U.S.-Russia rivalry in Iraq and Syria has also been exacerbated by the geopolitical implications of Operation Inherent Resolve. Russia's increased involvement in the region has been seen by some as a challenge to U.S. influence and a power play to expand Russian interests. The

U.S., on the other hand, has viewed Russia's actions with suspicion, questioning their true intentions and motives.

Furthermore, the U.S.-Russia rivalry has had significant implications for the humanitarian situation in Iraq and Syria. The ongoing conflict has resulted in the displacement of millions of people, with both countries accused of exacerbating the crisis through their military actions. The U.S. has faced criticism for civilian casualties resulting from aerial and drone strikes, while Russia has been accused of targeting civilian infrastructure and aiding the Assad regime in committing human rights abuses.

In conclusion, the U.S.-Russia rivalry in Iraq and Syria during Operation Inherent Resolve has been characterized by a mix of limited cooperation and frequent confrontations. While both countries share a common goal of defeating ISIS, their differing objectives and strategies have often led to tensions and challenges in coordinating efforts. The geopolitical implications, humanitarian consequences, and ethical considerations of this rivalry have had far-reaching effects on the overall dynamics of the conflict in the region. Historians studying this period will undoubtedly delve deeper into the intricacies of this rivalry and its impact on the broader Middle East region.

The Impact of Operation Inherent Resolve on Geopolitical Alliances in the Middle East

Title: The Impact of Operation Inherent Resolve on Geopolitical Alliances in the Middle East

Introduction:

Operation Inherent Resolve, the U.S. military intervention against ISIS in Iraq and Syria, has had profound implications for geopolitical alliances in the Middle East. Understanding these consequences is crucial for historians seeking to assess the effectiveness of coalition efforts and the broader impact on regional stability. This subchapter explores the complex dynamics and key factors that have shaped alliances during and after Operation Inherent Resolve.

Regional Stability and Geopolitical Alliances:

Operation Inherent Resolve has significantly influenced regional stability in the Middle East. Historians must analyze the evolving alliances between the United States and various regional actors, including Iraq, Syria, Turkey, Saudi Arabia, and Iran. The relationships between these states have been shaped by shared interests, conflicting objectives, and the need to combat the common threat of ISIS.

The Role of the U.S. Military in Combating ISIS Propaganda and Recruitment:

Historians must also examine the role of the U.S. military in countering ISIS propaganda and recruitment efforts. Through strategic communications, international partnerships, and technological advancements, the U.S. military has sought to undermine ISIS' ability to inspire and attract followers. Understanding these efforts is crucial for assessing the impact of Operation Inherent Resolve on the broader fight against extremism.

Effectiveness of Coalition Forces in Coordinating Efforts:

Analyzing the effectiveness of coalition forces in coordinating efforts against ISIS is essential for historians. This subchapter delves into the challenges faced by the coalition, such as diverse objectives, communication barriers, and operational coordination. Evaluating the successes and failures of coalition coordination provides valuable insights into the dynamics of multinational military campaigns.

Humanitarian Consequences on Displaced Populations:

Operation Inherent Resolve has had significant humanitarian consequences on displaced populations in Iraq and Syria. Historians must study the impact of military operations on civilian casualties, refugee flows, and the displacement of vulnerable communities. Assessing the response of coalition forces to these challenges sheds light on the ethical considerations surrounding military interventions.

Geopolitical Implications on U.S.-Russia Relations:

The geopolitical implications of Operation Inherent Resolve on U.S.-Russia relations in the Middle East are another crucial aspect for historians to explore. This subchapter examines the competition and cooperation between the two powers, their respective strategies, and the impact on regional dynamics. Understanding this complex relationship provides insights into the broader regional power struggles.

Conclusion:

Operation Inherent Resolve has had a multifaceted impact on geopolitical alliances in the Middle East. Historians must analyze the consequences for regional stability, coalition coordination, humanitarian efforts, and U.S.-Russia relations. By examining these aspects, a comprehensive understanding of the operation's impact on the Middle East can be achieved, contributing to informed historical analysis and lessons for future military interventions.

The Future of U.S.-Russia Relations in the Post-ISIS Era

As historians, it is crucial for us to analyze and understand the complex dynamics of U.S.-Russia relations in the post-ISIS era. The military intervention against ISIS in Iraq and Syria, known as Operation Inherent Resolve, has had significant geopolitical implications, particularly in the context of U.S.-Russia relations in the region.

Throughout the conflict, Russia has supported the Syrian government, while the United States has backed various rebel groups, leading to a clash of interests. However, both countries have shared a common goal in combating ISIS, which has allowed for some degree of cooperation and coordination.

In the aftermath of ISIS's territorial defeat, questions arise regarding the future of U.S.-Russia relations. Will the shared objective against ISIS pave the way for broader cooperation, or will it be overshadowed by other regional tensions and conflicts?

One major challenge is the divergent interests of the United States and Russia in the Middle East. While the United States seeks to promote stability and democracy, Russia aims to maintain its influence and support its ally, the Syrian government. These conflicting objectives have the potential to strain relations between the two powers.

Another factor to consider is the role of regional stability in shaping U.S.-Russia relations. The impact of Operation Inherent Resolve on regional stability in the Middle East is of paramount importance. Will the military intervention lead to a more secure and stable region, or will it exacerbate existing conflicts and power struggles?

Additionally, the humanitarian consequences of Operation Inherent Resolve cannot be overlooked. The displacement of populations in Iraq and Syria has created a significant humanitarian crisis. How the United States and Russia address these challenges will undoubtedly have an impact on their future relations.

Furthermore, the reconstruction and stabilization efforts in post-ISIS Iraq and Syria will play a crucial role. Will the United States and Russia cooperate in rebuilding these war-torn countries, or will their differing approaches hinder progress?

Ultimately, the future of U.S.-Russia relations in the post-ISIS era remains uncertain. The success of coalition coordination against ISIS in Iraq and Syria does not guarantee continued cooperation between the United States and Russia in the region. As historians, it is essential for us to closely monitor and analyze the evolving dynamics of this relationship and how it shapes the geopolitical landscape in the Middle East.

Chapter 8: The Role of Aerial and Drone Strikes in the Success of Operation Inherent Resolve against ISIS

Precision Strikes: Targeting Key ISIS Positions

Precision strikes have played a critical role in the success of Operation Inherent Resolve against ISIS in Iraq and Syria. By accurately targeting key ISIS positions, coalition forces have been able to significantly degrade the terrorist organization's capabilities and disrupt their operations.

These precision strikes have been conducted by a variety of means, including aerial bombardment and the use of unmanned drones. The U.S. military, in particular, has been at the forefront of employing these tactics to eliminate high-value targets and dismantle ISIS infrastructure.

One of the primary advantages of precision strikes is their ability to minimize collateral damage. By utilizing advanced targeting systems and intelligence gathering, coalition forces are able to identify and engage specific ISIS positions while avoiding unnecessary harm to civilians and critical infrastructure. This has greatly contributed to the overall effectiveness of Operation Inherent Resolve and has helped to mitigate humanitarian consequences on displaced populations in Iraq and Syria.

Furthermore, precision strikes have been instrumental in countering ISIS propaganda and recruitment efforts. By targeting key communication networks and media production facilities, coalition forces have disrupted the dissemination of extremist ideology and hindered the group's ability to recruit new members. This has significantly weakened ISIS's influence and outreach, making it more difficult for them to replenish their ranks.

However, the strategies employed by ISIS in response to precision strikes have also evolved. The terrorist organization has adapted to the increased threat and has resorted to dispersing their forces among civilian populations, using them as human shields to deter precision strikes. This has presented a complex challenge for coalition forces, as they must carefully balance the need to eliminate ISIS targets with the imperative to minimize civilian casualties.

In conclusion, precision strikes have proven to be a crucial component of Operation Inherent Resolve's success against ISIS in Iraq and Syria. By accurately targeting key positions, coalition forces have been able to disrupt ISIS operations, counter their propaganda efforts, and minimize collateral damage. While challenges remain, the continued use of precision strikes will be essential in defeating ISIS and ensuring regional stability in the Middle East.

The Utilization of Drones in Intelligence Gathering and Combat Operations

Drones have revolutionized modern warfare and intelligence gathering, playing a crucial role in Operation Inherent Resolve against ISIS in Iraq and Syria. This subchapter explores the utilization of drones by the U.S. military and coalition forces in their efforts to combat the terrorist organization.

In the realm of intelligence gathering, drones have provided unparalleled capabilities. Equipped with advanced surveillance technology, these unmanned aerial vehicles have been instrumental in locating and tracking ISIS militants. The ability to conduct real-time aerial reconnaissance has allowed military commanders to gather critical information on enemy positions, movements, and tactics, thus enhancing situational awareness and operational planning.

Moreover, drones have proven to be effective tools in combat operations against ISIS. Armed with precision-guided munitions, these unmanned aircraft have successfully targeted key ISIS infrastructure, including command and control centers, weapon depots, and training camps. By striking these targets with minimal collateral damage, drones have significantly weakened the capabilities of ISIS, disrupting their operations and degrading their combat effectiveness.

The use of drones has also minimized the risk to coalition forces. By conducting airstrikes remotely, military personnel can avoid putting their lives in immediate danger. This has been particularly valuable in the challenging and complex urban warfare environments of Iraq and Syria, where ISIS has sought refuge in densely populated areas. Drones have allowed for precise targeting, reducing the risk of civilian casualties and minimizing the potential for unintended consequences.

However, the utilization of drones in intelligence gathering and combat operations is not without its challenges. Technological limitations, such as limited flight endurance and vulnerability to electronic warfare, have necessitated continuous research and development to enhance drone capabilities. Additionally, ethical considerations surrounding targeted killings and the potential for misuse of this technology have sparked debates about the legal and moral implications of drone warfare.

Nonetheless, the successful integration of drones into Operation Inherent Resolve has undoubtedly contributed to its overall effectiveness. These unmanned aircraft have provided critical intelligence, facilitated precise strikes, and reduced the risk to coalition personnel. As historians, it is important to analyze and assess the impact of drone utilization on the outcomes of this military intervention, shedding light on the evolving nature of warfare and the ethical considerations that arise in the face of advancing technology.

The Controversy Surrounding Civilian Casualties and Collateral Damage

The U.S. military intervention in Iraq and Syria, known as Operation Inherent Resolve, has been a subject of intense debate and controversy. One of the most contentious issues surrounding this military campaign is the question of civilian casualties and collateral damage.

Historians studying Operation Inherent Resolve are keenly interested in understanding the extent of civilian harm caused by the coalition forces' military operations against ISIS. The impact of these casualties on the local population and the long-term consequences for regional stability in the Middle East are areas of particular concern.

While the coalition forces have taken measures to minimize civilian harm, there have been numerous reports and allegations of civilian casualties resulting from airstrikes and ground operations. Critics argue that the high number of civilian deaths undermines the legitimacy and effectiveness of the military campaign, as it risks alienating local populations and fueling anti-U.S. sentiment.

The U.S. military has maintained that it takes extraordinary precautions to avoid civilian casualties, employing advanced targeting technologies and conducting extensive intelligence assessments before launching any operation. However, the challenges of operating in densely populated urban areas, where ISIS fighters often hide among civilians, make it difficult to completely eliminate the risk.

Another aspect of the controversy surrounding civilian casualties is the issue of collateral damage. This refers to the unintentional destruction of civilian infrastructure, such as homes, schools, and hospitals, during military operations. Destruction of critical infrastructure not only leads to the displacement of populations but also hampers post-conflict reconstruction and stabilization efforts.

The legal and ethical considerations surrounding civilian casualties and collateral damage are of utmost importance. International humanitarian law prohibits the deliberate targeting of civilians and demands that all feasible precautions be taken to minimize harm to non-combatants. The U.S. military has faced scrutiny over allegations of violating these principles, and historians are interested in assessing the adherence to these laws during Operation Inherent Resolve.

Understanding the controversies and challenges surrounding civilian casualties and collateral damage during Operation Inherent Resolve is crucial for historians seeking to comprehensively evaluate the effectiveness and impact of the military intervention. It provides insights into the complexities of modern warfare, the ethical dilemmas faced by military forces, and the consequences for regional stability and post-conflict reconstruction efforts in Iraq and Syria.

Chapter 9: The Strategies Employed by ISIS in Response to Operation Inherent Resolve

Adapting to the Changing Military Landscape: ISIS Tactics and Countermeasures

The subchapter "Adapting to the Changing Military Landscape: ISIS Tactics and Countermeasures" delves into the evolving strategies employed by ISIS in response to Operation Inherent Resolve, the U.S. military intervention against ISIS in Iraq and Syria. This chapter explores the historical context and provides an analysis of the impact these tactics have had on the effectiveness of coalition forces in countering the threat posed by ISIS.

As historians, it is crucial to understand the ever-changing nature of warfare and the ability of militant groups like ISIS to adapt to new challenges. The subchapter explores the tactics employed by ISIS, ranging from conventional warfare to guerrilla tactics, suicide bombings, and the use of propaganda and recruitment efforts. By examining these tactics, historians gain valuable insights into the mindset and capabilities of ISIS, shedding light on the challenges faced by coalition forces.

Furthermore, this subchapter highlights the countermeasures implemented by coalition forces to neutralize the threat posed by ISIS. It assesses the effectiveness of these countermeasures, including targeted airstrikes, intelligence gathering, and the training and equipping of local security forces. By analyzing the successes and failures of these efforts, historians can evaluate the overall effectiveness of Operation Inherent Resolve and draw lessons for future military interventions.

The subchapter also explores the legal and ethical considerations surrounding the U.S. military intervention in Iraq and Syria during

Operation Inherent Resolve. It examines the challenges faced by coalition forces in navigating the complex web of international laws and norms governing armed conflict, as well as the ethical dilemmas inherent in combating a non-state actor like ISIS.

Ultimately, this subchapter provides historians with a comprehensive understanding of the ever-evolving military landscape and the strategies employed by ISIS in response to Operation Inherent Resolve. By examining the tactics and countermeasures employed by both sides, historians can draw valuable insights into the challenges faced by coalition forces, the impact of the intervention on regional stability, and the geopolitical implications of Operation Inherent Resolve on U.S.-Russia relations in the Middle East.

The Evolution of ISIS Propaganda and Recruitment Strategies

Introduction:

The subchapter "The Evolution of ISIS Propaganda and Recruitment Strategies" delves into the changing tactics employed by the Islamic State of Iraq and Syria (ISIS) in their propaganda and recruitment efforts. This chapter aims to provide historians and specialists in Operation Inherent Resolve with a comprehensive understanding of the evolution of ISIS propaganda and recruitment strategies, shedding light on the challenges faced by the U.S. military and coalition forces in countering these efforts.

Historical Context:

To comprehend the evolution of ISIS propaganda and recruitment strategies, it is crucial to examine the historical context that shaped their approach. The chapter explores the early days of ISIS, highlighting their effective utilization of social media platforms, such as Twitter and YouTube, to disseminate their extremist ideology and attract supporters globally. It also analyzes their strategic use of graphic violence and shock tactics to instill fear and gain attention.

Propaganda and Recruitment Strategies:

The subchapter then delves into the evolution of ISIS propaganda and recruitment strategies over time. It explores how the group adapted their tactics in response to the U.S.-led coalition's efforts, including Operation Inherent Resolve. This section examines the shift towards more sophisticated and targeted messaging, including the recruitment of foreign fighters, the radicalization of vulnerable individuals, and the exploitation of grievances and social media algorithms.

Countermeasures and Challenges:

The following section assesses the role of the U.S. military and coalition forces in combating ISIS propaganda and recruitment efforts. It analyzes the effectiveness of their strategies, such as psychological operations, cyber warfare, and partnerships with social media companies. The subchapter also highlights the challenges faced by these forces, including the rapid evolution of technology, encryption methods, and the resilience of ISIS networks.

Implications and Consequences:

Furthermore, this subchapter explores the geopolitical implications of ISIS propaganda and recruitment strategies in the context of U.S.-Russia relations and regional stability in the Middle East. It also examines the humanitarian consequences of these tactics, particularly the displacement of populations in Iraq and Syria.

Conclusion:

In conclusion, "The Evolution of ISIS Propaganda and Recruitment Strategies" subchapter provides a detailed analysis of the development and adaptation of ISIS propaganda and recruitment tactics. It addresses the challenges faced by coalition forces and the U.S. military in countering these efforts, while also highlighting the broader implications on regional stability, humanitarian consequences, and the legal and ethical considerations surrounding Operation Inherent Resolve. Historians and specialists in Operation Inherent Resolve will find this subchapter invaluable in understanding the multifaceted nature of the conflict and the ongoing fight against ISIS propaganda and recruitment.

Assessing the Resilience of ISIS in the Face of Coalition Pressure

Introduction:

This subchapter delves into the assessment of the resilience of ISIS (Islamic State of Iraq and Syria) in the face of the coalition's relentless pressure and efforts to eradicate the terrorist organization. By analyzing various factors, this chapter aims to provide historians with a comprehensive understanding of ISIS's ability to adapt and survive amidst overwhelming coalition coordination.

Resilience of ISIS:

ISIS, despite facing significant military pressure from the Operation Inherent Resolve coalition, has showcased a remarkable level of resilience. The organization's survival and ability to sustain its operations can be attributed to several key factors.

1. Adaptive Strategies: ISIS has displayed a remarkable ability to adapt its strategies in response to coalition pressure. The group has shifted from conventional warfare to a more decentralized and asymmetrical approach, utilizing guerrilla tactics, terrorist attacks, and exploiting social media platforms for recruitment and propaganda.

2. Propaganda and Recruitment: Despite coalition efforts to counter ISIS's propaganda and recruitment, the group has managed to maintain a significant online presence. Their ability to exploit social media platforms and disseminate extremist ideologies continues to attract vulnerable individuals, posing a long-term challenge for coalition forces.

3. Geopolitical Implications: The geopolitical implications of Operation Inherent Resolve have impacted U.S.-Russia relations in the region. The differing approaches and objectives of these two major powers have complicated the effectiveness of coalition efforts, allowing ISIS to exploit the resulting gaps and continue its operations.

4. Local Security Forces: The challenges faced by the U.S. military in training and equipping local security forces in Iraq and Syria have hindered the coalition's progress in eradicating ISIS. Insufficient resources, corruption, and political instability within these local forces have created setbacks, providing ISIS with opportunities to regroup and launch counteroffensives.

Conclusion:

Assessing the resilience of ISIS in the face of coalition pressure is crucial in understanding the complex dynamics at play in the fight against terrorism. Despite coalition efforts, ISIS has shown adaptability, particularly through the use of propaganda, recruitment, and the exploitation of geopolitical tensions. Addressing these challenges requires a comprehensive approach that not only focuses on military operations but also considers the social, political, and economic factors that contribute to the resilience of ISIS. By learning from the past, historians can contribute valuable insights into the ongoing struggle against ISIS and help shape more effective strategies for future efforts.

Chapter 10: The Impact of Operation Inherent Resolve on Reconstruction and Stabilization Efforts in Post-ISIS Iraq and Syria

Rebuilding Infrastructures: Challenges and Priorities

The subchapter "Rebuilding Infrastructures: Challenges and Priorities" delves into the complex task of rebuilding the devastated infrastructures of Iraq and Syria in the aftermath of the ISIS conflict. This chapter aims to provide historians and experts in various niches, such as Operation Inherent Resolve, regional stability in the Middle East, and the humanitarian consequences, with a comprehensive analysis of the challenges and priorities faced in the reconstruction and stabilization efforts.

One of the primary challenges in rebuilding infrastructures in Iraq and Syria is the extensive damage caused by the protracted conflict. The destruction of roads, bridges, hospitals, schools, and other vital infrastructure has severely crippled the affected areas. The widespread devastation demands a massive reconstruction effort that requires substantial financial resources, expertise, and coordination from both local and international actors.

However, amidst the challenges, certain priorities need to be addressed to ensure effective rebuilding. Firstly, the restoration of basic services such as electricity, water, and healthcare is crucial to improve living conditions for the displaced populations and facilitate their return to their homes. This requires targeted investments in rebuilding power plants, water treatment facilities, and medical infrastructure.

Secondly, the reconstruction efforts must prioritize the rehabilitation of key economic sectors. By revitalizing industries such as agriculture, manufacturing, and oil production, the local economy can rebound, providing employment opportunities and fostering stability. Additionally, the restoration of public transportation networks and communication systems is vital for the overall functioning of the region.

Another priority is the need for a coordinated approach among the various actors involved in the rebuilding process. The collaboration between local governments, international organizations, humanitarian agencies, and the military is crucial to ensure efficient resource allocation and avoid duplication of efforts. Effective coordination can also help address political, social, and ethnic tensions that may arise during the reconstruction phase.

Furthermore, the subchapter discusses the importance of incorporating local communities in the decision-making process. Engaging with local stakeholders and considering their needs and aspirations is instrumental in rebuilding trust, promoting social cohesion, and preventing the resurgence of extremist ideologies. Moreover, investing in education and vocational training programs can empower the local population and foster long-term stability.

In conclusion, the chapter "Rebuilding Infrastructures: Challenges and Priorities" highlights the immense challenges faced in reconstructing Iraq and Syria after the ISIS conflict. By addressing the challenges and prioritizing the restoration of basic services, economic sectors, and coordination efforts, the reconstruction and stabilization efforts can pave the way for a more stable and prosperous future in the region.

Political Stability and Governance in the Post-ISIS Era

Introduction:

The defeat of ISIS in Iraq and Syria marked a significant milestone in the global fight against terrorism. However, the aftermath of this military victory raised important questions regarding political stability and governance in the region. This subchapter explores the challenges and opportunities faced by the international community in establishing a stable political order in the post-ISIS era.

1. Transitioning from Military Intervention to Civilian Governance:

The success of Operation Inherent Resolve in defeating ISIS necessitates a smooth transition from military intervention to civilian governance. Historians will examine the effectiveness of the international community's efforts in establishing democratic institutions and promoting good governance in Iraq and Syria.

2. Rebuilding Trust and Reconciliation:

Operation Inherent Resolve not only focused on defeating ISIS militarily but also aimed to address the root causes of extremism. Historians will analyze the impact of this military intervention on regional stability, particularly in terms of rebuilding trust and promoting reconciliation among diverse ethnic and religious groups.

3. Local Security Forces and the Fight against Extremism:

One of the significant challenges faced by the U.S. military was training and equipping local security forces in Iraq and Syria. This subchapter will assess the effectiveness of these efforts in building capable and sustainable security institutions to prevent the resurgence of extremist groups.

4. Countering Propaganda and Recruitment:

ISIS relied heavily on propaganda and recruitment to spread its ideology and attract followers. Historians will evaluate the role played by the U.S. military in combating ISIS propaganda and recruitment efforts, particularly through the use of information warfare and counter-narratives.

5. Humanitarian Consequences and Displaced Populations:

The military intervention had profound humanitarian consequences, leading to the displacement of millions of people in Iraq and Syria. This subchapter will explore the challenges faced by the international community in providing humanitarian aid and supporting the reconstruction efforts in post-ISIS Iraq and Syria.

6. Geopolitical Implications and U.S.-Russia Relations:

Operation Inherent Resolve had significant geopolitical implications, particularly in terms of U.S.-Russia relations in the region. Historians will assess the impact of the military intervention on the complex dynamics between these two global powers and its implications for regional stability.

Conclusion:

The post-ISIS era presents both challenges and opportunities for political stability and governance in Iraq and Syria. Historians will critically analyze the strategies employed by the international community in countering extremism, rebuilding trust, and promoting good governance. This subchapter aims to provide a comprehensive assessment of the impact of Operation Inherent Resolve on political stability and governance in the region.

International Support and Assistance in the Reconstruction Process

The reconstruction and stabilization efforts in post-ISIS Iraq and Syria have been significantly supported by the international community. The devastating impact of the conflict and the widespread destruction left in the wake of ISIS's reign of terror necessitated a coordinated and comprehensive approach to rebuilding these war-torn nations. This subchapter will explore the international support and assistance provided during the reconstruction process, highlighting the collaborative efforts that have been made to restore stability and promote long-term peace.

One of the key contributors to the reconstruction process has been the coalition forces led by the United States under Operation Inherent Resolve. This multinational coalition has provided crucial military support, training, and expertise to local security forces, enabling them to regain control of territories previously held by ISIS. Moreover, the coalition has played a vital role in coordinating efforts among various actors, including humanitarian organizations, to ensure an efficient and effective response to the humanitarian crisis caused by the conflict.

International organizations such as the United Nations (UN) and the European Union (EU) have also played a significant role in supporting the reconstruction process. The UN has been actively involved in coordinating humanitarian aid, providing essential services to displaced populations, and facilitating the return of refugees and internally displaced persons to their homes. The EU has contributed substantial financial assistance to the reconstruction efforts, focusing on infrastructure development, governance, and capacity-building measures to ensure long-term stability.

Bilateral assistance from countries such as Canada, Germany, and the United Kingdom has been instrumental in addressing the immediate needs of the affected populations. These countries have provided humanitarian aid, funding for reconstruction projects, and technical assistance to enhance the capacity of local institutions. Additionally, regional actors like Saudi Arabia and the United Arab Emirates have contributed to the reconstruction efforts, recognizing the importance of stability in the region.

The support and assistance provided by the international community have been crucial in addressing the challenges faced in post-ISIS Iraq and Syria. However, it is essential to acknowledge that the reconstruction process is complex and multifaceted, requiring sustained commitment and resources. As historians, it is imperative to analyze the effectiveness of these international efforts, assess their impact on regional stability, and understand the geopolitical implications of Operation Inherent Resolve on U.S.-Russia relations in the region.

In conclusion, the international support and assistance in the reconstruction process have played a vital role in restoring stability and promoting long-term peace in post-ISIS Iraq and Syria. The collaborative efforts of the coalition forces, international organizations, and bilateral partners have contributed to addressing the humanitarian crisis, rebuilding infrastructure, and strengthening local institutions. However, challenges persist, and it is essential to evaluate the effectiveness of these efforts, considering the legal and ethical considerations surrounding the U.S. military intervention during Operation Inherent Resolve.

Chapter 11: The Legal and Ethical Considerations Surrounding the U.S. Military Intervention in Iraq and Syria during Operation Inherent Resolve

The Legitimacy of the U.S. Military Intervention under International Law

In the subchapter titled "The Legitimacy of the U.S. Military Intervention under International Law," it is imperative to delve into the legal and ethical considerations surrounding the U.S. military intervention in Iraq and Syria during Operation Inherent Resolve. Historians, as well as those interested in understanding the complexities of this intervention, will find this discussion crucial in assessing the overall effectiveness and consequences of the operation.

Under international law, the legitimacy of military interventions is determined by various factors such as self-defense, authorization from the United Nations Security Council, or consent from the host state. In the case of Operation Inherent Resolve, the U.S. military intervention was primarily justified under the concept of collective self-defense. The rise of ISIS posed a significant threat not only to the stability of Iraq and Syria but also to the broader Middle East region and international security. Therefore, the U.S. and its coalition partners argued that their military actions were necessary to protect their own interests and the interests of the international community.

Critics, however, question the legality of the intervention, arguing that it lacked explicit authorization from the United Nations Security Council or consent from the Syrian government. While it is true that the Security Council did not pass a resolution explicitly authorizing the intervention, the U.S. and its coalition partners argued that they were acting within the framework of existing Security Council resolutions, such as Resolution 2249, which called upon member states to take all necessary measures to combat ISIS.

Another legal consideration is the principle of proportionality. According to international humanitarian law, military interventions must be proportionate to the threat faced and must minimize harm to civilians. Operation Inherent Resolve employed precision airstrikes and targeted operations to minimize civilian casualties. However, there have been reports of civilian casualties, raising concerns about the extent to which the intervention adhered to the principle of proportionality.

Ethically, the U.S. military intervention raises questions about the responsibility to protect civilian populations and the long-term consequences of the operation. While the intervention aimed to combat ISIS and restore stability to Iraq and Syria, it also resulted in the displacement of millions of people and significant damage to infrastructure. Historians need to examine the ethical implications of these humanitarian consequences and assess the overall impact of Operation Inherent Resolve on the affected populations.

In conclusion, understanding the legality and ethical considerations surrounding the U.S. military intervention in Iraq and Syria during Operation Inherent Resolve is crucial for historians and those interested in comprehending the complexities of this intervention. By examining the justifications and legal frameworks employed, as well as the ethical implications and consequences, a comprehensive assessment of the operation's legitimacy can be made.

Human Rights Violations and Accountability in the Fight against ISIS

The subchapter titled "Human Rights Violations and Accountability in the Fight against ISIS" delves into the complex issue of maintaining human rights standards while combating the heinous acts of ISIS. This chapter aims to provide historians with an in-depth analysis of the challenges faced by coalition forces in upholding human rights, ensuring accountability, and seeking justice for the victims of ISIS.

Throughout the course of Operation Inherent Resolve, the U.S. military and its coalition partners encountered numerous instances of human rights violations committed by ISIS. These violations ranged from widespread atrocities, such as mass killings, sexual slavery, and the displacement of millions of civilians, to the destruction of cultural heritage sites. The chapter explores the strategies employed by ISIS in response to coalition efforts and their impact on human rights.

One of the key aspects discussed in this subchapter is the importance of accountability and justice in the fight against ISIS. Historians will gain insight into the various mechanisms established to hold perpetrators accountable for their actions, including international criminal tribunals and domestic courts in Iraq and Syria. The chapter will also examine the challenges faced in collecting evidence, ensuring witness protection, and facilitating the prosecution of individuals involved in human rights abuses.

Moreover, the subchapter delves into the legal and ethical considerations surrounding the U.S. military intervention in Iraq and Syria during Operation Inherent Resolve. It examines the justification for military action under international law, the adherence to rules of engagement, and the efforts made to minimize civilian casualties.

By addressing the issue of human rights violations and accountability, this subchapter contributes to the broader understanding of Operation Inherent Resolve and its impact on the affected regions. Historians will gain a comprehensive perspective on the challenges faced by coalition forces, the strategies employed by ISIS, and the legal and ethical dilemmas encountered during the fight against this extremist group.

Overall, this subchapter sheds light on the complex nature of the fight against ISIS and emphasizes the importance of upholding human rights, ensuring accountability, and seeking justice for the victims. It provides historians with a thorough analysis of the challenges faced by coalition forces while navigating the legal and ethical considerations in this multifaceted conflict.

Ethical Dilemmas Faced by U.S. Forces in Combatting ISIS

Introduction:

As the U.S. military intervened against ISIS in Iraq and Syria during Operation Inherent Resolve, it encountered numerous ethical dilemmas that tested the core values and principles of its forces. These dilemmas arose from the complex nature of the conflict, the tactics employed by ISIS, and the impact of military operations on civilian populations. This subchapter explores some of the key ethical challenges faced by the U.S. forces during their fight against ISIS.

Protection of Civilian Lives:

One of the primary ethical dilemmas faced by U.S. forces was the protection of civilian lives amidst the chaos of the conflict. As ISIS deliberately embedded itself within civilian populations, U.S. forces had to navigate a fine line between targeting enemy combatants and minimizing harm to innocent civilians. This necessitated strict adherence to the principles of proportionality and distinction, ensuring that the use of force was justified and civilian casualties were minimized.

Rules of Engagement:

The U.S. military also faced ethical dilemmas concerning its rules of engagement. Balancing the need for force protection and the prevention of civilian harm required careful decision-making. U.S. forces had to determine when to engage in combat, when to use lethal force, and when to exercise restraint, all while adhering to international humanitarian law. This required a delicate balance between achieving military objectives and upholding moral obligations.

Treatment of Detainees:

Another ethical challenge arose in the treatment of ISIS detainees. U.S. forces had to ensure that detainees were treated in accordance with international standards of human rights and were not subjected to torture or mistreatment. This meant maintaining humane conditions of detention and conducting fair and transparent legal processes. However, the difficulty of gathering intelligence from detainees while adhering to these standards posed a significant ethical dilemma.

Cultural Sensitivity:

The U.S. military had to navigate the complexities of cultural sensitivity while operating in Iraq and Syria. This involved understanding and respecting local customs, traditions, and religious beliefs to avoid inadvertently causing offense or alienating the local population. U.S. forces had to be aware of the potential impact of their actions on the perception of the mission and the broader regional stability.

Conclusion:

The U.S. forces faced numerous ethical dilemmas during Operation Inherent Resolve in their fight against ISIS. These challenges required careful consideration and decision-making to ensure the protection of civilian lives, adherence to rules of engagement, humane treatment of detainees, and cultural sensitivity. By addressing these ethical dilemmas, the U.S. military aimed to uphold its values and principles while effectively combating ISIS in Iraq and Syria.

www.ingramcontent.com/pod-product-compliance
Lightning Source LLC
Chambersburg PA
CBHW021801150726
47989CB00004B/1750